A Walled Garden in Moylough

A Walled Garden

in Moylough

Poems

Joan McBreen

Story Line Press | *Pasadena, CA*

ISBN 978-1-58654-063-0 (tradepaper)
      978-1-58654-077-7 (casebound)

The National Endowment for the Arts, the Los Angeles County Arts Commission,
the Ahmanson Foundation, the Dwight Stuart Youth Fund, the Max Factor Family
Foundation, the Pasadena Tournament of Roses Foundation, the Pasadena Arts &
Culture Commission and the City of Pasadena Cultural Affairs Division, the City of
Los Angeles Department of Cultural Affairs, the Audrey & Sydney Irmas Charitable
Foundation, the Kinder Morgan Foundation, the Meta & George Rosenberg
Foundation, the Allergan Foundation, the Riordan Foundation, Amazon Literary
Partnership, and the Mara W. Breech Foundation partially support Red Hen Press.

Second Edition
Published by Story Line Press
an imprint of Red Hen Press
www.redhen.org

Acknowledgements

Acknowledgements are made to the editors of the following publications in which many of these poems first appeared, sometimes in different forms: *Poetry Ireland Review; The Salmon Journal; Cyphers; Fortnight; The Honest Ulsterman; The Applegarth Review; Force 10; Colby Quarterly* Vol. 28, N-o. 4; *Riverine; La Collina Anno VIII/IX* – Numero 16/18 (Italy); *Woman's Way; The Sligo Champion; Writing in the West* (Connacht Tribune); *The Tuam Herald; The Great Tuam Annual; The Fiddlehead* (Canada); Grain (Canada); *Irish America; Westerly* (Australia); *Verse* (Scotland); *The Great Book of Ireland; The Mayo Anthology; The Humours of Galway; The Inward Eye* (Sligo Poetry Broadsheet); *Women's Work* (Wexford); *Under the Shadow—Westport Poetry Anthology; Irish Poetry Now—Other Voices; The Poet and the World—International Poetry Anthology* (Seattle, U.S.A.); *Cúirt Anthology No. I; Full Moon* (Killybegs Poetry Broadsheet); *U.C.G. Women's Studies Review* Vol. I, Vol. II; *Seneca Review* (U.S.A.) Vol. 23, Nos 1 and 2—(Special Issue, Irish Women Poets); *The Southern Review* (U.S.A.); *The Maryland Poetry Review* (U.SA.); *Ms. Chief; Irish Women's Review; Lifelines; Real Cool: Poems to Grow Up with; Mná na hEorpa Broadsheet* (International Women's Day 1993).

The poems in this collection are published in the U.S.A. by Story Line Press—an imprint of Red Hen Press. Thanks to RTÉ Radio and Television, Radio Kerry, Radio Ulster and BBC Radio 3 where many of these poems were broadcast between 1990 and 1994. Special thanks to John MacKenna, Seamus Hosey and Niall MacMonagle. My grateful thanks to the editor, Jessie Lendennie of *Salmon Poetry,* Galway, and also to Brenda Dermody of Poolbeg Group Services, Dublin, who designed the Irish edition cover. For her unfailing friendship, support and encouragement over many years, my thanks to my fellow Galway poet and broadcaster, Anne Kennedy, R.I.P.

I would like to thank Ailbhe Smyth, Director, Women's Studies Centre, UCD, for not alone using my work with her students and at conferences but for her continued help and comments.

To Listowel Writers' Week, The Yeats Society and The Poets' House, (Islandmagee, County Antrim), The Galway Writers' Workshop, The Killybegs Writers, and the many groups that I have had the privilege of working with, a special thanks.

My thanks to Declan Varley of *The Tuam Herald* who typed the original manuscript of this book; to Jim Carney and David Burke for their help and encouragement over the years, and also to Jane Prendergast and Breda Kenny.

I wish to thank Michael and Migi Reynolds, Moylough House, Moylough, County Galway.

My special thanks to Joe McBreen.

For Brian, Jody, Sarah,
Helen, Peter, and Adrian.

Contents

A Walled Garden in Moylough

Ben Bulben

In my childhood
winter was over
when snow streamed down
the face of Ben Bulben

and young women
seeking husbands
climbed the other hill
to place marriage stones on Maeve.

But stones are heartless things
useful for making walls.
Did Gráinne then, who fled
with her voluptuous lover

choose the finer way?
Was she safer
on the mountainside
than in a house of stone?

Lettergesh

It is April in Lettergesh. A man
wearing a blue cap mends his fence;
rain washes his brown hands
as he works. I am standing
between turf and door
among whin and stone.

He thinks of what he must do,
takes action, leans back,
inspects and works again,
as much making as mending;
slightly clumsy now, he
tosses bits of rusty wire away.

He walks a little to the right
and at a distance,
between the fence and himself,
removes his cap and wipes his face.
Mist rises from the grass, and as
rain sheets the mountain

dusk approaches. Behind me
is a room, a table
with a red-draped cloth, books,
papers, and a child's broken
toy, upended
on the floor.

Feathering the Room

Imagine the woman nesting in a room,
silence broken only by the hum of her sewing-machine
or continuous high-pitched whining of the dog
she keeps chained up all day.

Glancing at herself in the mirror, she lights fires,
dusts, settles photographs among plants
and red candles on the window sills.
Oh, think of a garden of pretty flowers!

Outside the air is still. Before flying south,
a swallow enters, perches on her shoulder;
she touches his feathers and kisses
her lover's letter. "Take it easy," she says,

"think of tomorrow." On the threshold
of the slightly open door she stands
warming the swallow near her breast,
a stone and a knife at her feet.

Tomorrow she may kill the swallow.
She is tired trying to bend her days,
days which have bent her as branches
in a forest they have owned.

When the swallow is dead, she will keep the feathers.

Rose Cottage Finisklin, c 1955

I am peeling potatoes for dinner, thinking
about this and that, a sun-filled orchard,
my mother and her friend under laburnums.

My mother's friend is washing in the old style,
wash, wash, wash, wring, rinse
like her mother and her grandmother.

In a barrel of rainwater near the kitchen
window-sill, her daughter washes her feet
while I whisper in the trees with my sister.

Thirty years from then my mother sits
with old photographs, wearing night clothes all day,
remembers liking jazz, faded films, Fred Astaire;

thinks of children in an apple orchard
and waits in silence for someone
to touch in passing an old woman's hair.

"Eanach Cuain"

January sunlight, blind half-drawn
down long classroom windows,
chalk-dust.

A child sings the old lament,
grace notes leave her throat,
clean, griefless.

Impossible to know which is remembered,
the haunted air, my mother's fingers
tightening on my arm

or the quickened beat
of the heart when the room was still
and filled with silence.

Dream of Poet and Child

You must believe me when I tell you
it is not because the room I write in
is sunlit or each window frames
a painting, that my dream returns.

I recall you leaning against a fence
in a cornfield, your arms
cradling a blond child, the blackness
of your hair making of his a golden moon.

I ascend the link chains easily,
glide over the top despite
the fullness of my long white dress.
In deep sleep I search

the endless space between us. But
where have you fled away to?
What is this darkness?
Why the salt taste on my lips?

When I reach the place
my fingers touch nothing
but damp and flattened grasses
where his and your body had been.

The Nest

At dusk we found it in the hedge,
four eggs like tiny speckled
marbles, still warm
when we held them in the palm
of our hands.

I threw one down, then another.

You laughed. I threw one more.
You passed me back the last to throw.

Splinters of shell, feathers, blood,
a yellow-streaked-with-green mess
lay in the middle of the tarred road.

We ran home through dark fields,
crossed gates.

All night I sucked my fingers.
A full moon outside my window
sat in a cold sky.

II

I sit here
in a half-lit room,
a black stain at my heart.

I am on an empty road.
The ditch is wrapped
in its own shadows,
a nest is full of bits of white down.

This Light, This Silence

If you tried to convince me sunlight
glinting from hedge to hedge
would cease to remind me
how we once moved from silence
to silence, I might not believe you.

Without you strange shadows
lurk at the foot of my bed.
When night settles down you flood
over me like the first breaking
of wet dawn.

The room I live in is empty.
Beyond my window I see in a country
house someone has lit a candle.
Its fragile brightness can be seen
miles away.

I need it to remind me of you,
the light little more than nothing
yet it marks my direction
like a bonfire burning.

A Walled Garden in Moylough

Now this May evening is quietly breathing
around us; your tobacco smoke swirls
in the stillness and I remember my lost father.

The wide street outside is silent.
Houses, shops and church are shuttered
and a light rain drifts in from farms and quiet fields.

The story begins: we are attentive to one another
knowing what we already know will be transformed
as a baby on its way transforms the young mother.

The evening darkens. The words we share lift clearly.

Inside our glasses are cooling on a low table.
In firelight we yearn for something nameless,
freely given as trees, meadows and frail bluebells.

I stand at the windows. The garden's lunar shadows
fall on white stone and juniper, and I know
my stillness is part of yours in the walled garden.

Moore Hall in September

It is a clear afternoon, warm in these woods.

there is your memory, a lake of events
at the edge of my mind, photographs
taken, days we walked with winter in the air.

Someone is felling trees in the distance,
another is skating on ice.

Once, men ran through these woods trembling;
one brought his wife home a hatful of eggs
unbroken from where he found them in the grass.

I have placed branches of the rowan,
hazel and beech in a black vase
and recall how I held the shrubs back
while you searched for something else.

The windows of the house are bricked in now
and there is no longer a roof. Autumn
is a heap of dead leaves on the great steps.

Someone Should Tell My Mother

Tonight my mother is walking in a bare room
over my head.

Someone should tell her to sleep now.

Tonight my mother is holding a skirtful
of apples warm against her breast.

Someone should tell her to eat now.

Tonight my mother is sewing a dress for me.
She cries out when the needle pierces her hand.

Someone should tell her how helpless I am.

Tonight I will tell my mother she must
leave me alone, but wait, I cannot.

I hear a rustling sound coming from the room

like someone sifting through hundreds of pages
seeking a happy ending and the sound is like the sea

which is very far away.

Bog Cotton

The fields are drenched with it,
feather-down heads, gossamer
on stalks both hardy and frail.
Nothing breaks the silence
in a Roundstone bog
but a curlew's cry caught in the wind.

The mist clears; I pass a woman
standing on a grass verge,
smiling, talking to herself.
Wet grass anoints her ankles,
her voice falters, drifts.

Behind a wall horses grow restless,
seagulls clamour overhead
and the woman is silent,
I walk to the end of Inishnee
where shadows fall on rocks and shore

and the sun shines on *ceannabhán*,
mysterious, *uaigneach*.

ceannabhán   bog cotton
uaigneach   lonely

In the Daughter's Room

My grandmother is coughing in her sleep
in the room next to mine.
I am in the dark listening to trees
behind the house sway in the wind.
My mother tiptoes past.

I make a tent of my blankets
so that I will not hear the rain
turn to sleet on the window.

I am dreaming of you in white, running
on bare feet over the hills or moving
with me in the grass, barely breathing.

I have disappeared from the room,
the garden, the street and this house
to a place where I cannot be found, but still
hear the sound of others searching for me.

After Osip Mandelstam

From now on dark begins at four
and letters pile up like old wood.
       Coffee will turn grey in cups.
       It will be night endlessly.

The sun was so bright on the beach
yesterday when I was out tramping.
       It was cold. The sea left
       little corpses in the wrack.

My window looks on the pines
at the back of the garden.
       It is raining. Listen, I hear
       a kind of sobbing.

The Mountain Ash

If you can imagine it
fully grown, red berries
in clusters on every branch,
and if you understand
my desire to tend it
always in my own place,
you will know why I carried
it here as a sapling,
uncovered the roots from plastic,
exposed them to the cold air.

This sheltered garden
will never resemble
its wild hills nor the soil
deceive as black earth
of the mountain, yet
I can be seduced into believing
my mountain ash
will live, and day after day
draw me to the window,
allow me rise with certainty.

I carry my washing in and out
in great armfuls,
bring a necessary stake
to my mountain ash when it struggles
against the harsher winds.

Blind with sleet, on days I cannot
see my face in the mirror
it comforts me as neither child
nor lover could. I planted it.
Without me it will die.

Girl

A girl in a red skirt
leaps through the bog.
Her bare feet leave
prints on the rocks.

Now she crouches
near a thorn bush
sheltering from the rain.

And my heart
has kept her all these years
like a stranger.

The Mahogany Mirror in
My Mother's Room

And there you were on a clear summer morning
holding a peach nightgown against you,
your body reflected in the mahogany mirror
in your room, eyes examining
lace and silk, oblivious of mine
watching you from the middle of your bed.

Walking Barefoot on White Feathers

The mother walks barefoot on a ring
of white feathers, arms outstretched
under blue skies, clouds and apples;
above the garden, asleep, swing angels.

Brown trees after storms appear
to listen, but trees and angels
do not absorb tears
nor the din of far-off screams.

She warns her child that angels
make no sound. The day is ordinary;
the child who stumbles
on feathers and apples, weeps.

"I will work at my weaving to please you,"
she says, "I will make music
with the noise of my loom."
Clack and whirr, whirr and clack.

Once she knelt veiled in a dark church,
invoked saints and gods to dispel her tormented
dreams, as her candle, ignited in its own paper cup,
dissolved before her eyes.

Lifting her into her arms,
the mother puts on the child's red shoes;
together they kneel
in the meadow of long grass.

The Little Street

(after Vermeer, Rijksmuseum, Amsterdam)

I

She is sitting with her sewing in an open door,
the dark behind her.

Although the little street is quiet and still,
she is not alone.

The girl-child she watches over
plays with her dog, motionless in the heat

and her friend, sister or neighbour
washes her hands in the rain barrel.

All are in their own light and shadow.
There is no speech between them.

(My shadows have returned, encircling me
in this space. I turn away).

II

My grandmother, wearing black, is sitting
on a kitchen chair outside our front door.

My mother is standing at the stove, wiping
tears from her eyes, about to call out.

I am wearing no shoes. It is summer
and there are daisies in the wet grass.

And now as I remember it, a man
is stumbling down the little street,

squinting in the sun, saying something
we can almost hear. We have all turned away.

Woman Watching the Door

I am walking in an orchard with my mother.
She is naming the apple trees as we pass:
Cox Pippin and Beauty of Bath.

She stoops to fasten the strap of my sandal,
sunlight the colour of leaves in her hair.

We made our way from one year to another,
to my children around her
in an over-heated room, her eyes dim.

Someone carries a tea-tray towards her
as the winter light fades outside.

She neither eats nor weeps
but watches the door,
as a woman in a dry field waits
for someone to give her passage beyond.

The Clean Slice

Beyond the garden's solitude
is the dark shore, hills and wind.
A mantle covers somebody passing
with a lantern. He turns, looks back
and in the house where he lived
sleep his wife, his children.
He drops his lantern, the light goes out,
light that once fell as warm shadows
in a summer garden on sunburnt hands
and arms, on a woman's hair. In darkness
he hears their voices grow faint,
give way to silence, broken only
by the harsh sound of his son cutting
bread, the clean slice through the crust.

In the Brief Time Given

I stand by the table, making rules
for my child, his hand on the fruit,
his eyes looking beyond me through the window
at the trees and the bird tuning up.

I tell him not to put shoes on the table,
bring hawthorn indoors, break mirrors
or open umbrellas in the house.

Rain pours on lilacs in the yard
and I shelter him with myself.
Then I get on with the morning wash,
the child leaving me to it, taking with him
into the distance images of secret and threat,
alive to what my words said
and did not say, in the brief time given.

Watches

A man sits in a sunlit garden.
Birds swoop over the feeding table,
crying, scavenging.

He has sent for the jeweller.
Two suitcases of watches
are brought to him.

How pale and thin
the man has become, skin
around his wrists wrinkled and dry

yet his fingers rummage
desperately through the pile.
He chooses his new watch.

The birds fly into the air.
Time passes. The weather
turns.

Now the watch rests
on the bedside table
with the man's pipe, glasses, empty shoes.

On Hearing My Daughter
Play "The Swan"

My daughter plays Saint-Saëns. It is evening
and spring. Suddenly I am outside
a half-opened door. I am six years old
but I already know there's a kind
of music that can destroy.

My mother is playing a waltz, Chopin,
and everything is possible. There are lilacs
in a vase on the hall table, white among
the colourful umbrellas, folded,
full of the morning's light rain.

My sisters' voices are calling one another
far down the street. There are wind-blown leaves
under my father's feet as he enters the room.
I look at him as if for the first time
and he grows old.

I see my mother rise from the piano
and close it gently. She takes a glass
from the table. It is empty. But she has put
a weight in me, the weight of something
that has died in her.

As my daughter sustains the melody
with her right hand, the tumult
of the chords she uses with her left hand
brings into the room
the hush and roar of the sea.

Heart in a Black Bowl

I once had a lover, a golden man.
In the city he betrayed me, was lost in the crowd.
Then there was nothing but a copper sky
and my heart encased in iron. In a black bowl
I carried it to the window-sill in winter.

A bottle of red wine contained my lover.
It was like this: apples and wedges of lemon
on a table, blue cornflowers and wheaten bread,
his face turned towards me, white, desiring.

As he drifted from me, I turned to my mirror.
These eyes know me, the woman I was for him,
I loved him yet he flew from my hands
like seeds or feathers and found his place
in the dark earth.

The Photograph of My Aunts

The photograph I found beneath the purple box
must have been lost and left behind.
It shows two sisters wearing white lace
in late summertime.

Goats graze under lilac trees. Two older women
wearing straw hats, stitch in pink and blue
tiny knitted garments; their dresses blow in a breeze
that lifts the edges, revealing black button boots.

The sisters near the window-frame
have hair blown in a hazy lane.
This portrait stares from my wall,
the faces haunt me with other likenesses.

It hangs over the piano
near the painting of an apple orchard.
The sisters are dead.
In the photograph they wear white shoes.

They lean against the warm wall of the house.

Possibilities

In times that have no present
we stick to the images of old memories.
                              Ivo Smoldas

Orpen's washerwoman in deep shadows,
arms bare, hair in curls,
speaks to her companion in low tones.

A friend leans against the wall
of an orange beach hut, dreaming
under an indigo sky.

Baudelaire's eyes are fixed on the distance.
Your handwriting faces towards
my bedroom mirror.

The words merge into one another. You wrote:
"We have come so far, only this far."

In this familiar room I have drawn
curtains back onto
an unbearable white morning.

One yellow beech leaf spirals downwards.
How slowly it is falling. Evergreens
move, an intricate dance arrangement.

My children's feet crunch on the gravel path.
The present is still possible, a world
clear as the voices outside, the past

a collection of postcards, a photograph I have kept.

Woman Herding Cattle
in a Field near Kilcolgan

Whenever I see her
in my mind's eye
I see her squat body in a crossover apron
and boots, calmly walking her field.

The spring night has come on,
taken me unawares and the lane is dark out there.
I think of her alone beside the hearth,
the radio turned on.

Whenever bare branches
turn again to leaf,
I will remember her
walking quietly in a sunlit space.

I will think of the woman
herding cattle in a field near Kilcolgan
alive with herself, company
for sheep and cows.

When I wake in the night
I see her too, young
and light-haired,
running in a green field.

Veronica

I

Veronica's maidservant scrubs the floor.

Her washing heavy on her hip, Veronica
goes to the river where singing women
beat hempen clothes on stones.

Plunging her hands into cold water,
watching them redden, grow coarse,
she remembers once being told death
by drowning is like strangulation.

Noon, and a dead cat lies sprawled
in the dust.

Finished her chores, the maidservant
lurking in shadows hides her face beneath lace.

Veronica lingers by the river, dreaming
of March in the garden, the hard hot earth,
smell of oranges and grass.

II

Her kitchen is dim. Herbs dangle
from the rafters, copper pans on the walls
are campfires in candlelight.

The maidservant in threading a needle
with grey-blue wool.
Veronica is at the table, her floury hands
knead dough.

It is not this she thinks about, but the outline
of a face on white cloth, the way it moved
in the breeze when she hung it
on the clothesline in the garden,

how it caressed her arms.

Snow in September

If you think only of me
imagine when
you opened the curtains wide,
dimmed the light,

hooked your right arm
over my bare shoulder,
traced with your fingers
on my face, moved

from the small space
beneath my ears
to softly touch my mouth,
and it snowed outside.

My hands sweated
on the cold window-ledge
and I shivered, for I wore
only your thin shirt.

While the snow-world whitened
and swirled, your hands
curled about tea I brought you
in a blue cup.

I placed my left arm
along the length of your body
and you said hoarsely
"I think only of you."

On Reading Your Letter in June

June and the hedges are drenched with hawthorn.
It is evening. There is a silken rustle
in the beeches. I sit with your letter; the wind makes
the whispering sound of lovers' laughter;

laughing I wore a blue dress at the water's edge,
your fingers stretched out to touch me. Nothing
kept me from you. In the morning there was
lavender on the window-sill and to this I return;

returning each time to find it startles like something
that is itself. Nearly midnight, I stand
in the open doorway. I speak to you
but your back is turned. You are painting a picture;

picturing a stone cottage, alone and exposed.
Two people have arrived from another place
over a bridge. You have painted trees the colour of rust.
You sign the painting with your name,

your name that no longer catches in my throat.
Look at you wrapping yourself up in your dark coat.
See how the trees have darkened. The town lights
have come on and each house holds a woman.

The two in the painting survive. I finish your letter.

In a Suburban Garden on Christmas Night

It is late. The night has turned to frost;
in the shadow of thickish trees
a swing stands to attention and a cat scuttles
past my ankles in search of heat and sleep.

Without saying anything, you left
and do you know I miss you?

You who used to call every day.

The garden darkens and a light snow falls.
Its flakes melt on my hair, my eyes, my mouth.

Inside a child cries over a lost toy soldier.
His cardboard universe stands still,
all its scenes played out.

You, I miss, my friend who left
without saying anything.

The Silken Robe

I grow weary of mourning you,
winding your hair around my hands,
dressing and undressing, wide awake
or semi-conscious, my face touching
your face, my arm resting on your thigh.

Cover me with your silken robe,
cool against my skin
in the heat of summer, warm
when I whisper of cold.

Cold, that in the candlelight I carry
to illuminate your face,
brings ice to the roots of my hair.

The Iris Garden

High over the harbour
we are in the iris garden;
all the others are in the glass room
bending towards one another.

We speak of how soon
you will be with us
not raising our voices above
a whisper; you are the breath between us.

Our blue dresses move gently.
There are only two irises
open to the sun and they lean
against a wall, are naked.

Our eyes are shut but not sleeping.
We tell each other how little
we remember even when we were awake
and it was morning.

The sea is groaning down below,
ebbing, flowing and carrying
its wrack to the shore; we know
and we imagine you there, almost.

The Inner Room

I

It is quiet in the inner room.
I wear a white dress
with a black rose pinned on it.

I keep the doors closed.
Although the window allows
in the sun, I am cold.

There is movement
however imperceptible in the garden,
life or a lover sneaking away.

II

The trees are coming into leaf.
To be comfortable I have unfastened my dress.
Standing in the doorway I'm dreaming.

I've turned my back to you . . .
My spirit has wandered into the sky.
But who will understand this?

III

I will leave my shoes empty on the doorstep
and be glad in the sun,

I will travel beyond the gates and join
you and that other one

and when the house lights yellow the dusk
beginning to show over the town,
I will look forward to the birth of stars
before I lie down.

IV

Sometimes I have a dream:
I am in a great forest seeking
childhood's half-forgotten tales.

I am lost in high mountains
seeking the air-castles
of my girlhood.

But in your arms losing my way
is impossible, for I have followed
you dumbfounded and amazed.

V

Everything can happen without me,
landscapes cloud over, skies
remain seamless,
downpours continue,

all as it should be
coping with no help from me.

VI

In every house a woman works
a ball of knitting wool.
One is afraid, for she is in another place,
not here where all the others are.

She is holding out her hand
to catch a thread which is stretching
around a corner.

She is offered nothing back. There is a labyrinth
she must enter over there.

VII

I left my light blue dress
of the sky's colour
on a rock beside the sea
and in my nakedness you caressed me.

All day I sat at your table
and drank wine from a deep glass
in silence.

Yet happiness is far away,
in a grave
where a man lies.

Hanging Wallpaper

It has gone on all morning.
Scrape, scrape, tear, strip,
the sound is in my head,

I am clenching my teeth,
it is inside my belly
until I cannot bear it any longer.

I am in a room
on the other side of the wall.
I stretch my legs out under a table.

They feel like someone else's
excavated from a pit.
But wait. The scraping has ceased.

Frost in the garden, half-starved birds,
dead flowers. The leaves are falling,
the old wallpaper is falling.

Time to hang the new,
choose the colour quickly—pink, blue?

Fionnuala

Imagine the bell's call
in a town asleep
beneath bleak mountains,

a woman alone in a room,
a vase with blossoms,
scentless things.

The dark sky
shadows a space,
the white page,

rage of winter
in the alders
and Lir's daughter,

a swan in waters
wilder, deeper
than she's ever known,

laments and laments again.

The Notebook

First entry. Girl in gingham, red.
Older girl in white, floating silk.

Second entry. Nun in black,
chalk. Tonic sol-fa.

Third entry. Middle room.
First Communion class. Laburnums.

Then a darkness. One day
talents were named.

We stood in a semi-circle.
All had one, some many.

Fourth entry. My turn.

Kindness. That was it.
I was called a strange name.

Fifth entry. What did it mean?

I wore a brown dress.
My face crumbled. I begged.

Sixth entry. Made alone in corner
of bedroom.

Sacred Heart looked down
over His red oil lamp. I wept.

Winding the Wool

She unplaited the figure-of-eight shape
of the skein and stretched it wide
apart, suddenly taut in her arms.

She placed it over my small upturned hands
and we sat face to face,
while she started to wind it in a ball.

Wool moved from here to there, the thread
running from my fingers quickly,
like rain streaming on the window pane.

The final inches slipped away from me
and she dropped her newly wound ball
on the floor. She worked the end
taken from me into her first stitches.

Hands still in my lap, I sat on a wicker
chair. Shadows from the fire
danced strangely on the wall
behind her head. I watched the thread.

In Memoriam J.P.B.

(1916–1993)

Death in April

Whenever I think
of Spring, such fragility
returns with wind-blown blossom.

Keeping Watch

She is silently
watching the flames transfigure
her face in the coals.

Night

Candle set in stone
spreads legendary shadows
over your new grave.

August

Beautiful country
on the rim of a hostile
sun winding into this heart.

Winter

See the ruined sky,
distant landscape that is burning
everything I loved.

The Lost Brooch

Newport, Co. Mayo, August 1993.

As I remember it,
there were oak trees
on both sides of a gravel
path, the stones were wet.

We had not sought shelter,
only tea and talk
in Newport House,
its windows open, beckoning.

There was no such welcome,
being a festival day
in the small town, visitors
of all kind around.

Through stalls and barrows,
oysters, balloons and painted faces,
we wove a steady path,
found a coffee shop and then

you entered with your friend
whose name, Hazel, reminded me
of childhood, a lake,
a wood, my white bicycle, plain bread.

"And what is it you've lost?"
I eyed you warily and reached
across my breast, my gaze
never leaving your face.

You held it out to me
in all its round, moon-gold glory,
the hooped brooch bought in Amsterdam,
a lover's gift, a pledge.

I took it from you, examined
the weakened pin. Sunlight
filled the place, encircled us.
We drank our tea, later wine

and time became an acorn
in a green case, floating
on a river in full flood
rising, falling before our eyes.

One for Sorrow

One magpie rests on a winter bush.
Crows scavenge a stubble field.

From where I am I cannot see or hear you.
The train moves west. You disappear.
Yet the wool I feel beneath my fingers
is the wool of your coat.

You stood outside the door,
shaded your eyes and said
"the blackbird, it's the blackbird I hear!"

Notes for American Readers

"Eanach Cuain" page 17
"Eanach Cuain" or "Eanach Dhúin" is a famous lament composed by
the blind poet Antoine Ó Raifteirí.
It refers to a drowning tragedy which occurred in 1828 in Eanach
Dhúin (Annaghdown), a townland in Galway where 20 people
travelling to Galway on the *Caisleán Nua* were drowned when a sheep
put its foot through the floor of the boat.

Biographical Note

Joan McBreen is from Sligo, Ireland, and now divides her time between Tuam and Renvyle, Connemara, Co. Galway.

McBreen's poetry collections are *Map and Atlas* (Salmon Poetry, 2017), *Heather Island* (Salmon Poetry, 2009, reprinted 2013), *Winter in the Eye – New and Selected Poems* (Salmon Poetry, 2003), *A Walled Garden in Moylough* (Story Line Press, 2020, and Salmon Poetry, 1995), and *The Wind Beyond the Wall* (Story Line Press, 1990, reprinted 2020). Her two anthologies are *The White Page / An Bhileog Bhán – Twentieth-Century Irish Women Poets* (Salmon Poetry, 2001) and *The Watchful Heart – A New Generation of Irish poets - Poems and Essays* (Salmon Poetry, 2001).

In 2014, she produced a CD *The Mountain Ash in Connemara – Selected Poems* by Joan McBreen with music composed and arranged by Glen Austin and performed by the RTÉ Contempo String Quartet. In 2015, she brought out a limited edition broadside *The Mountain Ash* in collaboration with printmaker artist, Margaret Irwin West, and printmaker, Mary Plunkett. It was designed and published by Artisan House Connemara.

McBreen has given readings and talks in universities in the USA including Emory, Villanova, De Paul (Chicago), Cleveland, Lenoir-Rhyne, N.C., and the University of Missouri-St. Louis. Since 2010, she has undertaken a number of reading tours in the US and has read in Nebraska, Iowa, Minnesota, Alabama, Kentucky, Georgia, and Massachusetts. She is closely associated with most of the major literary festivals in Ireland.

Joan McBreen was awarded an MA from University College, Dublin in 1997. Some of her papers are in the Stuart A. Rose Manuscript, Archives, & Rare Book Library at Emory University, Atlanta, GA.

CPSIA information can be obtained
at www.ICGtesting.com
Printed in the USA
JSHW040659151220
10254JS00001B/19

9 781586 540630